Chapter one from the clothbound book, "The Ruin of a Christian." Copyright 1944 by Sword of the Lord Publishers. Chapter two from the book, "The Soul-Winner's Fire." Copyright 1941 by Moody Bible Institute of Chicago.

GW00418416

Chapter 1

THE SEVEN-FOLD SIN OF THOSE WHO DO NOT WIN SOULS

1. *The Sin of Disobedience to Christ*
2. *The Sin of Little Love for Christ*
3. *The Sin of Not Following Christ*
4. *The Sin of Not Abiding in Christ*
5. *The Sin of Dishonesty in a Sacred Trust*
6. *The Sin of the Short-Sighted Fool*
7. *The Sin of Blood-Guilt—the Manslaughter of Souls!*

*T*HE WINNING of souls to trust in Jesus Christ and be saved from their sins is the principal duty of every Christian in the world.

That is the thing nearest to the heart of God. For this He sent His Son, Jesus Christ, into the world to live a sinless life and die on the cross. Jesus said, "I came not to call the righteous, but sinners to repentance" (Luke 5:32). And Paul said in I Timothy 1:15, "This is a faithful saying, and worthy of all acceptation, that Christ Jesus came into the world TO SAVE SINNERS!" And even now, in Heaven, "joy shall be in heaven over one sinner that repenteth, more than over ninety and nine just persons, which need no repentance" (Luke 15:7). The thing nearest to the heart of God is the winning of precious souls. It is the thing Christ died for. It

SOUL WINNING

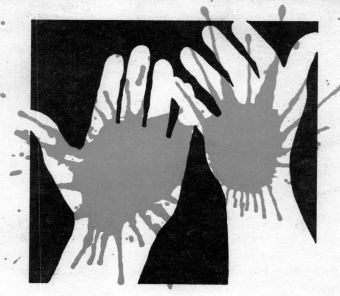

Bloody hands, the sevenfold sin of
not winning souls, and **how to cleanse
them** through God's way of soul winning.

John R. Rice

is the one great matter of rejoicing in Heaven. It ought to be the unceasing, principal business of every Christian.

The preachers in the New Testament churches were set on winning souls. Every one of them did the work of an evangelist, covering the Roman Empire with millions of believers in the first century after Christ died!

The ministry of Jesus was largely one of personal soul winning. He won Nicodemus one night. He won the woman at the well of Sychar in Samaria. He won the woman taken in adultery in the eighth chapter of John. He won the woman who was a sinner who wept over His feet at the home of Simon the Pharisee. He won the Gadarene demoniac, Mary Magdalene, and the woman who stooped to touch the hem of His garment in a throng. He won Zacchaeus, the publican, and Levi, another of the same kind. It was His daily business.

Soul winning was the normal thing for every individual Christian in Bible times. John the Baptist pointed Andrew and John to Jesus. Then Andrew won Peter. Jesus won Philip, then Philip won Nathaniel. The woman at the well of Sychar, a new convert, won many in her own town, the same day she was saved. The jailer at Philippi found Christ at midnight, and before morning had his whole family saved and baptized! When persecution began at Jerusalem, scattering all except the preachers, then "they that were scattered abroad went every where preaching the word" (Acts 8:4).

The Bible makes it clear that soul winning is the business of every Christian. One who does not win souls is guilty of a horrible list of sins which block revival, deaden the churches, grieve the Spirit of God, cause Christians to miss the joy and manifestation of the Holy Spirit, and damn millions of souls! Consider the seven terrible sins of every Christian who does not win souls as he ought.

1. The Sin of Disobedience to Christ

Christ plainly commanded every Christian to win souls. His Great Commission as given in Matthew 28:18–20 says:
"All power is given unto me in heaven and in earth. Go ye therefore, and teach all nations, baptizing them in the name of the Father, and of the Son, and of the Holy Ghost: Teaching them to observe all things whatsoever I have com-

3

manded you: and, lo, I am with you alway, even unto the end of the world."

To these eleven disciples Jesus explained that all authority was His, and that therefore they were commanded to go and make disciples in all nations, winning souls and getting them baptized. But it is obvious that eleven disciples could not win souls in every nation. The commission as given in Mark 16:15 says, "Go ye into all the world, and preach the gospel to every creature." To preach the gospel to every creature in all nations, even to the end of the world, was obviously more than those eleven disciples could do. They were simply to begin this work, doing what they could, then others were to carry it on.

And that is exactly what these eleven disciples were commanded to teach others. After they made disciples (got people to trust in Christ and be saved) and got them baptized, they were to continue, "teaching *them* to observe all things whatsoever I have commanded *you.*" They were to teach the new converts to set out to carry out the Great Commission *just exactly as the apostles were commanded to do it.* That means that every Christian in the world has exactly the same command as the apostles had, *to get people saved!* Every newborn soul ought to be taught to observe all things whatsoever Jesus commanded the apostles to observe, as the plain words of the Great Commission say.

So Jesus commands every Christian to win souls. Every Christian is equally responsible for taking the gospel to every creature.

This command is repeated again in the last chapter of the Bible. In Revelation 22:16, 17 Jesus Himself gives this plain command:

"*I Jesus have sent mine angel to testify unto you these things in the churches. I am the root and the offspring of David, and the bright and morning star. And the Spirit and the bride say, Come. And let him that heareth say, Come. And let him that is athirst come. And whosoever will, let him take the water of life freely.*"

Jesus plainly said He had sent His angel to testify unto us in the churches, "And let him that heareth say, Come."

Everyone who hears the gospel is commanded to tell lost sinners to come!

If you are not a soul winner, then, you are not obeying Jesus Christ, the One to whom all authority is given in Heaven and earth. You are not carrying out His commands. You are a disobedient child of God, if child of God you are. You are a rebel. However much money you give, however well you may teach the Bible, no matter how separated and unworldly you are in your life, you are not right in your heart; you are disobeying Christ if you are not a soul winner.

Remember that for disobedience and rebellion, Saul lost his kingdom, and he and his house were rejected by the Lord. God had the prophet Samuel say to Saul, "Hath the Lord as great delight in burnt offerings and sacrifices, as in obeying the voice of the Lord? Behold, to obey is better than sacrifice, and to hearken than the fat of rams. For rebellion is as the sin of witchcraft, and stubbornness is as iniquity and idolatry. Because thou hast rejected the word of the Lord, he hath also rejected thee from being king" (I Sam. 15:22, 23). No sacrifice you can make will be pleasing to God as long as you disobey Him. Rebellion is as the sin of witchcraft, stubbornness is as iniquity and idolatry. The sin of not winning souls is a sin of direct disobedience to the main command of Jesus Christ. It is disobedience of the last command Jesus gave His people before He went away. It is disobedience in the matter that is nearest to His heart. Oh, wicked sinners that we are, when we Christians do not win souls!

2. It Is the Sin of Lack of Love for Christ

Those who do not win souls as they ought are disobedient Christians, but that is not all. Their disobedience proves their lack of love for Christ.

In John 14:15, Jesus said to the same apostles to whom He first gave the Great Commission, "If ye love me, keep my commandments." And then in John 14:23, the same night He was betrayed, Jesus continued, "If a man love me, he will keep my words." Then in the next verse, John 14:24, Jesus said, "He that loveth me not keepeth not my sayings: and the word which ye hear is not mine, but the Father's which sent me."

5

There it is as clear as it can be, that if you love Christ you will obey Him, you will keep His words. If you love the Father, you will keep these words, because they are really the words of the Father as well as of the Son. Disobedience is evidence of lack of love.

All of us can well be ashamed that we do not love our Saviour better. But those who love the Saviour best are the best soul winners. Those who win fewer souls and work less at winning souls, love the Saviour less. Those who do not win any souls to Christ at all love Him, oh, so poorly! For Jesus Himself plainly said, "If a man love me, he will keep my words," and again, "He that loveth me not keepeth not my sayings."

In Dallas, Texas, I was called, at about 3:00 in the morning, to the bedside of a dying saint. "Daddy Hickman," with cancer of the liver, was about to go to meet his Saviour. He called his grown sons to his bedside, and took their hands and asked them a solemn question, one after another; "Son, are you going to meet me in Heaven? You can't tell me a lie on my deathbed, and I must know!" One by one the boys promised that they would take Christ as Saviour then and there, or declared that they had done so already and would live for Him. They made other holy promises. And I remember how moved one young couple related to the family were, when he called them and placed their hands together and solemnly urged them to quarrel no more but to have peace and a happy home.

How solemn are the parting words of a loved one! How earnestly we would take to heart the last command of a dying father! But how much more earnestly we should take to heart the last command of Jesus Christ, to go and preach the Gospel to sinners, to make disciples, to win souls.

Many a young man has all his life avoided the gambling table or alcoholic drinks because he promised a dear mother on her deathbed, and felt he must keep his promise. A late king of England read the Bible every day because he promised his mother, Queen Victoria, that he would. He loved his mother and so he could not ignore that sacred request. And if we love Jesus Christ we cannot ignore the plain command, the last entreaty of His heart, to go after poor lost sinners for whom He died and for whom His heart yearns, even yet, with inexpressible longing and love!

If you, then, do not win souls, your love for Christ has grown cold. Perhaps once you loved sinners, prayed for them, warned them and plead with them, but now you, like the church at Ephesus, have lost your first love. You do not win souls. Evangelists sometimes become "Bible teachers" because their love for Christ has grown cold. And Christians everywhere content themselves with the mere outward forms of worship and giving and praying and reading and doing "church work" when they ought to be winning souls. Oh, the trouble is, they are guilty of the sin of little love for Christ. For, "If a man love me,he will keep my words," Jesus said.

Do you love Christ? If you do, then you will win souls. If you make small effort to win souls, then your love is small. If you make none, how can you say you love Him at all?

3. It Is the Sin of Not Following Christ

In Matthew 4:19 Jesus said, "Follow me, and I will make you fishers of men." In Mark 1:17 Jesus said, "Come ye after me, and I will make you to become fishers of men." These promises were made to the apostles, but remember, He has given us the same commission, command and promise.

This matter of following Jesus, being a disciple or learner of His ways, is a matter often mentioned in His teaching in the Gospels. In Luke 9:23 Jesus said, "If any man will come after me, let him deny himself, and take up his cross daily, and follow me." And to the rich young ruler who thought he had kept the law from his youth, Jesus said, "If thou wilt be perfect, go and sell that thou hast, and give to the poor, and thou shalt have treasure in heaven: AND COME AND FOLLOW ME" (Matt. 19:21). We are to have the mind of Christ (Phil. 2:5). And I Peter 2:21 tells us, "For even hereunto were ye called: because Christ also suffered for us, leaving us an example, that ye should follow his steps." In John 12:26 Jesus said, "If any man serve me, let him follow me," and in John 14:12 we are promised that one who believes in Christ, "The works that I do shall he do also." So every Christian ought to follow Christ. But if you are not winning souls you are not following Christ. For He plainly says in Matthew 4:19, "Follow me, and I will make you fishers of men." The one who fails to win souls is sinning in the matter of not following Christ.

As a boy preacher I went with a dear old pastor through one summer, singing in five or six short country revival campaigns. When I started out to preaching I found I used some of the same texts and illustrations and ideas he did. Later I went with an evangelist to sing in one or two campaigns, and I learned all I could from him and used his methods and some of his sermon material. I was later assistant pastor to a godly man, a fine preacher, and to this day I acknowledge his help in many of my sermons. I followed these men, and so learned to do the work as they did it. One of the best ways to be an evangelist is to go with an evangelist and learn how he does it. But the very best way to be a soul winner is to follow Jesus, the Master Soul Winner, and get His passion, His burden for dying sinners, and be led by His Holy Spirit in winning them. No one really follows Jesus except as he becomes a soul winner. Jesus makes every true disciple, every learner, every one who follows in His steps, into a soul winner something like Himself.

If you, then, are not a soul winner, you are not following Jesus. What a sin!

4. Not to Win Souls Means That You Are Not Abiding in Christ

In John 15:1–8, the Lord Jesus gave a precious teaching about fruit bearing. Christ Himself is the true vine, and we are His branches. He said, "Every branch in me that beareth not fruit he taketh away: and every branch that beareth fruit, he purgeth it, that it may bring forth more fruit." You see, the idea is that every Christian should be in such close touch with Christ that, as the sap comes from the vine into the branch with life-giving, fruit-bearing power, so the Holy Spirit may flow from Christ through us, making us fruit-bearing Christians, really making us soul winners.

Again He said, "*Abide in me, and I in you. As the branch cannot bear fruit of itself, except it abide in the vine; no more can ye, except ye abide in me. I am the vine, ye are the* branches: *He that abideth in me, and I in him, the same bringeth forth much fruit: for without me ye can do nothing.*"—John 15:4, 5. There is no way to win souls except by abiding in Christ, being in touch with Him, knowing His will, feeling His heartbeat, being wholly committed to His will and work! But every one that really abides in Christ brings forth fruit, yea, much fruit! "He that abideth in me, and I in him, the same bringeth forth much fruit." In the same chapter verse 8 says, "Herein is my Father glorified, that ye bear much fruit; so shall ye be my disciples."

Remember that the Lord Jesus wants souls saved. That is what He died for. That is what preaching the gospel is for. That is what the Great Commission means. That is the work of the churches. That is what preachers are called to do. That is what every Christian is commanded to do. Christ 'came to seek and to save that which was lost.' "Christ Jesus came into the world to save sinners." If I abide in Christ, my aim, my purpose, my burden, my business, my work, will be that same precious work. And my fruit will be that same precious fruit. Soul winning is the business for which every Christian is called. Precious souls are the fruit we should bear. The fruit of a Christian is another Christian.

If you are not a soul winner, then the Bible makes it clear that you do not abide in Christ. Your heart is not at one with His heart. Whatever your activity, whatever your reputation, however sanctimonious you feel and however much of a Pharisee you are in your life, *you do not abide in Christ, if you do not win souls!* What a sin for a Christian not to abide with surrendered heart and perfect union, and so help in His blessed and main business of winning souls!

5. Not to Win Souls Is the Sin of Dishonesty in a Sacred Trust

In Matthew 25:14–30 is the parable of the talents. There the Saviour illustrated His own coming and kingdom in the future by the story of a man who had gone into a far country and left his affairs in the hands of his own servants. To one he had given five talents, to another two, to another one talent. And you remember that the first two men doubled the money left with them by trading; the third man hid his talent in the

9

earth, accusing his lord of reaping where he had not sown. But his master answered the servant, "Thou wicked and slothful servant . . . . Thou oughtest therefore to have put my money to the exchangers, and then at my coming I should have received mine own with usury." In the similar parable of the pounds in Luke 19:11-27, Jesus told how a lord went away to receive for himself a kingdom. First he gave his ten pounds to ten servants, saying to them, "Occupy till I come." When he returned, as Jesus will one day return, he called to them for an accounting. Again one man had laid up his pound in a napkin and had no increase, and Jesus called him, "Thou wicked servant"!

The idea in each case is that Jesus has given us His affairs for which we are to care. As honest stewards of that committed to our care, we must bring fruit; we must win souls. Every man who has received the gospel and all the blessings of salvation and has not passed them on is wicked, dishonest—a servant who has robbed his master of the proper increase he has a right to expect for his investment. Those whose pounds multiplied were to rule with their lord when he returned. How guilty was the wicked man who cheated his lord and had no increase to bring! So every Christian who does not win souls is a dishonest servant, and will face Christ with shame.

Sometimes we hear of the frightful scandal of a man who has been made executor of a will and stolen the funds he handled. Some man before his death appointed a friend to administer his estate, and to see that his widow and his orphan children were properly cared for. But the unfaithful administrator has been known to use the money for his own ends, or to waste it in speculation. Sometimes the widow lives in poverty, and the children, instead of being provided for as the father intended, must leave school. The administrator who wastes the estate committed to his hand, or who uses it for his own selfish gain, is a crook, a thief, a dishonest man. And that is exactly the kind of person a Christian is who takes salvation, takes all the blessings that God gives him freely, and then, instead of passing them on to others as he has been commanded to do, makes his Christian life only a matter of his own safety and comfort and blessing, and never wins the souls for whom Christ died! How wicked, how dishonest is the Christian who is an unfaithful steward of the gospel!

But the sin of the Christian who does not win souls is also dishonesty toward *men*. Paul said, "I am debtor both to the Greeks, and to the Barbarians; both to the wise, and to the unwise. So, as much as in me is, I am ready to preach the gospel to you that are at Rome also" (Rom. 1:14, 15). Paul was a man, one of a race of men. Paul could not wash his hands of his fellow men. Every man that lives owes something to the race. Every child receives from mother and father more than he can ever pay them. If he pays his debt at all it must be to the rest of the world. It is only a murderer like Cain who can say, "Am I my brother's keeper?" We owe a debt to every poor dying sinner! We are crooked, dishonest, unfaithful to a trust, if we do not share with others the precious gospel we have.

Dr. H. A. Ironside in 1943 was in Dallas, and in a letter to me enclosed a circular announcing his engagements in a number of colored churches with striking names. Across the top of the circular Dr. Ironside simply wrote, "Trying to pay my debt to my colored brethren." Every Christian has a debt to sinners. He has received that which is not his alone. If he selfishly takes for himself all the blessings of God he receives and does not lead others to know Jesus and have peace and forgiveness and a home in Heaven, if he does not keep others out of the torments of Hell, he is a dishonest man, an unfaithful steward, a wicked sinner against both God and man!

6. Not to Win Souls Is the Sin of a Short-Sighted Fool

These are strong words, but consider the words of the Scripture and see if they are not true. Proverbs 11:30 says, "The fruit of the righteous is a tree of life; and he that winneth souls is wise." Christians should bear fruit as a tree of life, and every wise Christian wins souls.

The same thing is taught in Daniel 12:2, 3 which says:

"And many of them that sleep in the dust of the earth shall awake, some to everlasting life, and some to shame and everlasting contempt. And they that be wise shall shine as

11

the brightness of the firmament; and they that turn many to righteousness as the stars forever and ever."

Oh, the bright shining of soul winners in Heaven! They that turn many to righteousness shall shine "as the stars forever and ever." Here we see that the true wisdom takes the long look. A Christian who has any spiritual wisdom can see it is not best to center his endeavors on things that pass away with his life. To make money, to make friends, to enjoy the pleasures of life—to be much concerned about these passing pleasures and this passing wealth is not good sense. It is not spiritual wisdom. When "them that sleep in the dust of the earth shall awake," when Christians come before Christ to receive their awards, when God's bonfire burns up the wood, hay and stubble of wasted lives, then every Christian who did not win souls will find that he has played the consummate fool!

Psalms 53:1 says, "The fool hath said in his heart, There is no God." No Christian can be that kind of a fool. Jesus said to the two disciples on the way to Emmaus, "O fools, and slow of heart to believe all that the prophets have spoken." These were Christians, but they were guilty of a kindred folly to that of the atheist. And the Christian who never wins souls is a fool, too, and for a very similar reason. The man who denies God and eternity is a fool. The man who does not believe the Bible is a fool. And so the man who lives as if this world were the only world; as if it were better to make money than to win souls; as if it were more important to fill his belly and clothe his back and live in a fine home and drive a nice car and make a name for himself, than to lay up treasures, and meet there in Heaven a host of those he has won to Christ, that man is a fool!

Oh, the short-sighted folly of those who neglect eternal things for temporal things! Oh, the sin of those who do not accept the value that Christ put upon a soul! Oh, how wicked is the sin of us poor foolish Christians who do not win souls and thus who miss the chance to shine forever and rejoice forever with the heart of the Saviour we have made so glad, by bringing sinners for whom He died to love and trust Him and be saved!

12

7. Not to Win Souls Is the Sin of Blood-Guilt; the Sin of Soul-Manslaughter

In Ezekiel 3:17–19, the word of the Lord came to Ezekiel, saying:

"Son of man, I have made thee a watchman unto the house of Israel: therefore hear the word at my mouth, and give them warning from me. When I say unto the wicked, Thou shalt surely die; and thou givest him not warning, nor speakest to warn the wicked from his wicked way, to save his life; the same wicked man shall die in his iniquity; but HIS BLOOD WILL I REQUIRE AT THINE HAND. Yet if thou warn the wicked, and he turn not from his wickedness, nor from his wicked way, he shall die in his iniquity; BUT THOU HAST DELIVERED THY SOUL."

If Ezekiel did not warn the Israelites about their iniquity, and if they died in their sins, then God required their blood at the hand of Ezekiel! What a staggering thought is this, that God says to a man about sinners, "His blood will I require at thine hand"! But if Ezekiel warned the wicked, even if the wicked did not turn, then God said, "Thou hast delivered thy soul."

That strange commission was given to Ezekiel for the nation Israel. Surely it implies that God still holds people to account for the souls of those that they do not warn! Surely we are guilty of the blood of every poor lost soul who goes to Hell if we had a chance to warn them, to weep over them, to woo them tenderly and win them and get them to come to Christ, and we did not!

Paul had this in mind when he came to Miletus, the little port of the great city Ephesus, and had the elders of Ephesus meet him there. Solemnly facing these preachers, Paul told them that after his three years' ministry in Ephesus they would see his face no more, and then said, "Wherefore I take you to record this day, that I am pure from the blood of all men. For I have not shunned to declare unto you all the counsel of God" (Acts 20:26, 27). Then he said again, "Therefore watch, and remember, that by the space of three years I ceased not to warn every one night and day with tears" (Acts 20:31).

13

Paul could solemnly say, 'After three years in Ephesus I am not to blame if any person here goes to Hell. I have no blood on my hands! I have gone night and day with tears, publicly and from house to house, carrying the whole counsel of God. I am not to blame if anybody goes to Hell!'

O Christian, is there blood on your hands? Are you guilty of the death of immortal souls for whom Christ died, because you did not warn them?

A missionary to China tells how, when a boat overturned in a Chinese river, he urged some near-by Chinese fishermen to bring their boat quickly and help him rescue a man who was struggling, drowning. The fishermen said it was none of their business. "How much?" they asked. They insisted on a price of fifty dollars before they would rescue the drowning man. The missionary gave them all the money he had, about forty dollars, and at last persuaded them to try to rescue the drowning man, but when he was brought out of the water it was too late. Life had already fled. The callous hearts of the fishermen took no responsibility for their drowning country-man. But they were guilty of murder, as certain as there is a God in Heaven to hold men to account!

But are you much different, Christian, when you let people near you go to Hell and you never warn them, never weep over them, never see that they have the gospel?

In Roosevelt, Oklahoma, I promised to go see a dying woman who was distressed about her soul. But I waited until the second day, and she died before I ever saw her. In Dallas, Texas, an old man, past eighty, heard me on the radio and wrote, saying, "I am dying with cancer and I am not ready to die. Brother Rice, please come and pray with me and help me to get ready to die." But I had so many burdens each day I postponed it, and finally after two weeks I sent a young preacher to visit the old man and help him prepare to meet God. When no one answered the doorbell a neighbor came to tell the young preacher that the old man had died and the family were then gone to his funeral! I have hopes that in their extremity these two people may have turned to the Lord and may have trusted Him. I say I have some hopes, but no certainty at all. And oh, what will I say to the Lord Jesus when I see Him, if He asks me to give an account for the

14

souls of these two who sent for me and I did not get there in time!

The sin of not winning souls is the sin, the blood-guilty, terrible sin of soul-manslaughter. I beg you in Jesus' name, consider how guilty you must be in God's sight if you do not put your very best and all your heart's strength and love into the one precious business of soul winning!

So, Christian, if you do not win souls, you are not right with God. You may be saved, but you are not a good disciple. You are a backslider. You may be born into God's family, but you are a poor, disobedient, wilful child. If you are God's child you are a disobedient one. If you are God's servant you are an unfaithful one. If you follow the Saviour at all, you follow afar off.

Consider again, this seven-fold sin of failing to win souls. It is the sin of disobedience, of lack of love, of failing to follow Christ, of not abiding in Christ, the sin of dishonesty in a sacred trust, a sin of short-sighted folly, missing eternal rewards, and a sin of blood-guilt for which we must give an account!

May God convict His people of their sin in not winning souls dying all around us.

Chapter 2

GOD'S WAY IN SOUL WINNING

"He that goeth forth and weepeth, bearing pre-cious seed, shall doubtless come again with re-joicing, bringing his sheaves with him."
—Psalm 126:6.

SOUL WINNING IS THE main business of a Christian. The saving of sinners is the thing nearest to the heart of God. For that purpose Christ came to earth, and lived and died and rose again. Even now the angels in Heaven rejoice more over one sinner that repents than over ninety-nine just persons that need no repentance. Soul winning is the eternal business. One sows now. and then reaps throughout the endless ages of glory, when he gives the gospel to sinners.

How may I win souls? That should be the chief concern of every child of God. The Scripture says, "Let him that heareth say, Come." And the Great Commission is given to every Christian that he should go into all the world and make disciples.

The Bible has much to say about how to win souls. Here in Psalm 126:6, God's way of winning souls is clearly laid out. A meditation on this passage, directed by the Holy Spirit, should certainly make clear God's infallible method in the winning of souls.

This is a psalm of revival:

"When the Lord turned again the captivity of Zion, we were like them that dream. Then was our mouth filled with laughter, and our tongue with singing: then said they among the heathen, The Lord hath done great things for them. The Lord hath done great things for us; whereof we are glad. Turn again our captivity, O Lord, as the streams in the south. They that sow in tears shall reap in joy. He that goeth forth and weepeth, bearing precious seed, shall doubtless come again with rejoicing, bringing his sheaves with him."

16

"When the Lord turned again the captivity of Zion, we were like them that dream." The captivity referred to must be the Babylonian captivity. We do not know the author of this psalm, but we know it is inspired by God. David wrote many psalms, Solomon, Moses, Asaph and others wrote some. The inspired writer here recalls the happy revival when the remnant under Nehemiah and Ezra returned from Babylon to build again the walls of Jerusalem and the Temple. It seemed too good to be true—it was almost like a happy dream when God turned the captivity of Zion.

Then their mouths were filled with happy laughter. It was not frivolous laughter, but the deep, joyous laughter so close to tears, so close to the shouting of praise. I have never yet broken out into uncontrollable shouting of praise, but sometimes I have been so happy that I could not refrain from laughter. So Sarah must have felt when God gave her the promised boy in her old age and she called him Isaac, "Laughter!" Many of us look back with mingled joy and longing to the times of great revival and blessing, when our mouths were filled with laughter and our tongues with singing.

"Then said they among the heathen, The Lord hath done great things for them. The Lord *hath* done great things for us; whereof we are glad." The heathen were impressed with the marvelous deliverance which God gave His people. Real, Heaven-sent revivals are like that. Outsiders know when God has visited His people. A great moving of repentance among the people of God, of tears, of restitution and reformation, times of joy and blessing and reconciliation, make a profound impression upon a community round about. Such had been the revival to which the Psalmist here refers, and then his heart cries out to God for a return of revival. "Turn again our captivity, O Lord, as the streams in the south."

Beware of Spiritual Bondage

There are other captivities worse than being carried into Babylon. Our churches are cold, our hearts are cold, our prayers are cold. The Bible becomes a dull Book. The ministry becomes a thankless task—a burden to be borne. Our services become mere form, our songs are meaningless. We feel the parching drought of worldliness. Our souls long for a breath from Heaven. We need a rain of the Holy Spirit upon God's people. We are carried captive by our sins and are crushed by the world about us. O God, turn our captivity again!

The Psalmist prays a big prayer and asks for a great revival. He prays, "Turn again our captivity, O Lord, as the streams in the south." He has in mind possibly the Nile River, rising in Lake Tana in Ethiopia and then flowing down through the hills to the broad plains of Egypt, where every year, until conquered by the British dam, it overflowed all the banks and watered the lowland. It irrigated the valleys and enriched the soil with overwhelming flood-tides of resistless water! May God send that kind of revival! As the song says,

> Mercy drops round us are falling,
> But for the showers we plead.

The Psalmist may have had in mind the Euphrates and Tigris Rivers, great broad streams that flow together and then sweep majestically on southeastward to empty their mighty burden into the Persian Gulf. We need to pray for and expect and try to have revivals that are as mighty as "the streams in the south."

"They that sow in tears shall reap in joy," the Scripture says. Revivals and soul winning are always matters of sowing and reaping. It costs to be a soul winner. Soul winning should be a matter of the deepest concern. If a soul winner is willing to sow in tears, he will certainly be able to reap in joy.

In verse 6, we have a clear outline of God's way to win souls and the certainty of results: "He that goeth forth and weepeth, bearing precious seed, shall doubtless come again with rejoicing, bringing his sheaves with him."

Analyze that verse and you will find these five parts in God's plan of soul winning:

1. "He that goeth forth"—the GO in soul winning.
2. "And weepeth"—the BROKEN HEART in soul winning.
3. "Bearing precious seed"—the WORD OF GOD in soul winning.
4. "Shall doubtless come again . . . bringing his sheaves

with him"—the CERTAINTY OF RESULTS with God's method.

5. "Rejoicing . . . bringing his sheaves with him"—the JOY OF THE REAPERS, or a soul-winner's reward.

The "Go" in Soul Winning

God's Word puts going as the first requirement in soul winning. How like the Great Commission, when Jesus said, "Go ye into all the world" (Mark 16:15), and again, "Go ye therefore" (Matt. 28:19). The main reason Christians do not win souls is that they simply do not get at it. The one who wins souls is the one who tries to win souls, the one who talks to sinners, the one who makes it his business.

Many have the impression that the best man or woman is the best soul winner—that the Christian who has the highest moral standards, pays his debts, avoids worldliness, attends church, tithes, etc., will automatically be the best soul winner; but that is not true. If it were true, then every Pharisee would have been a wonderful soul winner, but they were not. And many a Christian today prays, reads his Bible, attends church and carefully watches his daily life, yet never wins a soul. That is tragic, but true.

How often in revivals a good sister or brother rises to testify and says, "I want to live such a godly life that sinners will see my daily walk and be saved!" The fact is, their living a godly life does not win sinners to Christ. That is not the way God has appointed to get sinners saved. Living a godly life is important, vitally important, for the one who would be a soul winner, but the first condition of soul winning, divinely appointed, is this—get up and go after sinners!

Soul winners ought to know the Bible, but the best Bible students are often not the best soul winners. Many, many times in revivals I have noticed that preachers would sit in the services, enjoy the sermons, pray in public and show an active interest, but they would win very few sinners to Christ. The average preacher is not a good personal soul winner. But in the same revival I have seen many, many times a young person who had not been long converted, who knew little about the Bible and had little time to grow in Christian grace, yet who persistently and earnestly went after his friends until he won far more souls than the preachers. I have known a fifteen-year-old girl to win more souls in a revival than a half-dozen sincere preachers, and the reason was that she obeyed the command of the Scriptures to go after that which was lost. If you want to be a soul winner the first thing to do is to "go!"

I have known mothers and fathers to see their unsaved children grow up in the midst of prayers, Bible reading and moral teaching, and yet never once earnestly, lovingly, and persistently press the matter of definite and immediate decision for Christ. Among the hundreds of sinners I have dealt with, no cases are sadder than the unsaved sons and daughters of ministers. Young people tell me how they were accustomed to family prayer in the home and how they believed with all their heart in the sincerity of mother's and father's faith; yet it would seem that mother and father never went after their children for definite and immediate decision. There is no possible substitute for the "go" in soul winning. Doubtless Paul the Apostle was the greatest of all the apostles, and his greatness lay most of all, I think, in that, as he himself said, he was "in labours more abundant."

Do not get the idea that soul winning is a matter of talent. People do not win souls because they are educated, because they are peculiarly fitted by nature for it, because of a magnetic personality, or for any such reason. Those Christians who win the most souls are those who most persistently and with the greatest abandon go after sinners.

We must realize that soul winning is not done in human power and human wisdom. It takes the power of the Holy Spirit to convict and to convert a sinner. But remember that Jesus said, "Go . . . and, lo, I am with you alway, even unto the end of the world" (Matt. 28:19, 20). The obedient heart who sets about the Master's business, obeying His plain command to win souls, is far more likely to have the power of the Holy Spirit upon him, soul-winning power. Going is God's first requirement for soul winning.

One who would win souls must "be instant in season, out of season" (II Tim. 4:2). The best soul winners are those who go when it is convenient and then go when it is not convenient. "Blessed are ye that sow beside all waters" (Isa.
20

32:20). That is just another way of saying, "Blessed is the soul winner that tries to reach every sinner possible." Again, "He that observeth the wind shall not sow; and he that regardeth the clouds shall not reap" (Eccl. 11:4). You may think you do not know enough Scripture to win souls, but in a few minutes you can learn John 3:16, and that has led to thousands of conversions. Learn it and go! You may feel you do not know what to say. Ask God to give you the message and go! You may not know to whom you should speak first, but if in loving obedience you go, the Holy Spirit will direct your steps and your words. "He that goeth forth" is the one who will win souls.

It is said that in the last years of the war between the states, a farmer was drafted into the Confederate army. He did not know the drill manual. He did not know how to keep step on the march, nor how to salute. He knew none of the bugle calls. But he brought his squirrel rifle and when the command was given to attack he charged the Yankee lines, joining in the rebel yell. However, the gray-coated Confederates were outnumbered and were soon driven back. The bugle blew "retreat" and the thin gray line withdrew to safer ground. As the battered soldiers treated their wounded, prepared their camp and threw up breastworks in the late afternoon, some one said, "Poor old Jim! He was either killed or taken prisoner in the first battle he was in! Too bad he didn't know the bugle call to retreat and ran right into that nest of Yankees." But about sundown they saw two tired fellows coming over the hill. The one in front had on a blue uniform and the man behind wore a gray. Somebody had taken a prisoner! As he saw the camp, he prodded his prisoner with a bayonet and somebody shouted, "It is Jim! It is Jim! Jim's got a prisoner! Where did you get him, Jim?" The farmer recruit drew up angrily. He felt they had all deserted him in the first battle! "Where did I get him?" he said. "Why, the woods are full of them! Why don't you get one yourself?" So the world is full of sinners, and you can take them alive for Christ, if only you go after them.

My dear Christian friends, somewhere near you is a poor, lost soul, someone who would listen to you, someone who is burdened, someone who realizes he needs Christ. That soul is not saved because nobody has gone to tell him the message of salvation. "Go" is the first command of God to the soul winner. "He that goeth forth" is the man who returns with sheaves. If you want to be a soul winner then commit yourself to this holy business and go after sinners. Other things are necessary, but this is most necessary. If you would be a winner of souls, then you must go forth.

The Broken Heart in Soul Winning

"He that goeth forth and weepeth," the Psalmist says, will come back with sheaves, rejoicing. Beyond all doubt, this is another essential for the soul winner. If going forth is the first requirement of a soul winner, perhaps even the going involves a broken heart. If we care as we ought, we will go. A broken heart will send us forth.

It is amazing that we have few tears when there is so much to weep about. Have you ever felt the compassion that Jesus had as He looked on the multitude? Have you ever experienced what was in His heart as He wept over Jerusalem, and said, "O Jerusalem, Jerusalem, thou that killest the prophets, and stonest them which are sent unto thee, how often would I have gathered thy children together, even as a hen gathereth her chickens under her wings, and ye would not"? The love of the shepherd for the lost sheep, the tender compassion of the father for his prodigal son, exemplify the broken heart of God and of Christ over sinners. If we are to win souls as we ought, we must go, weeping.

Sometimes preachers are ashamed to weep; more often our hearts are too cold to weep over sinners. It was not so with Paul. To the assembled elders of Ephesus, Paul urgently said, "Therefore watch, and remember, that by the space of three years I ceased not to warn every one night and day with tears" (Acts 20:31). Paul warned people night and day. In verse 20 of the same chapter, he declares that he taught "publickly, and from house to house." Paul went forth to win souls publicly and from house to house, night and day. He put the "Go" in soul winning. But best of all, he went with tears! They that sow in tears shall reap in joy, and he that goeth forth and weepeth is the one who will come back rejoicing with sheaves.

22

Often I am amazed at the callousness of my own heart. How strangely absorbed we become in the things about us until we have little concern about souls to be eternally blessed or to be eternally tormented!

> Would you care if some friend
> You had met day by day
> Should never be told about Jesus?
> Are you willing that he
> In the judgment should say,
> "No one ever told me of Jesus?"

When I first began preaching, I remember how I wept from the beginning to the end of my sermons. I was embarrassed about it. This was wholly unlike the college debating, the commencement addresses and other public speaking to which I had been accustomed. The tears flowed down my cheeks almost continually, and I was so broken up that sometimes I could scarcely talk. Then I grew ashamed of my tears and longed to speak more logically. As I recall, I asked the Lord to give me better control of myself as I preached. My tears soon vanished and I found I had only the dry husk of preaching left. Then I begged God to give me again the broken heart, the concern, even if it meant tears in public, and a trembling voice. I feel the same need today. We preachers ought to cry out like Jeremiah, "Oh that my head were waters, and mine eyes a fountain of tears, that I might weep day and night for the slain of the daughter of my people!" (Jer. 9:1).

The personal soul winner needs a broken heart. The cold and callous sinner can, it may be, answer all your arguments and withstand all your pleas, but he has no argument against tears. If you have a holy compassion that is given of God, wrought by the Holy Spirit in your heart, until tears flow down your face as you talk to sinners, then you have a magnet that must tug at the heart of the coldest and hardest of unbelievers. After all, nothing can prove you and your message better than a love like Christ had for sinners. It is not hard to believe that God so loved the world, that He gave His Son, if those of us who tell about it have some of the same love to transform our appeal and give urgency to our message. May God give us tears!

Do You Care for the Dying?

After all, humanly speaking, there must be a multitude who are unsaved because no one especially cares. Many a man has felt in his heart the cry of the Psalmist, "No man cared for my soul!" A college senior told me, weeping, after I had just won him to Christ, "Nobody seemed to care whether I was saved or not!" It is one of the standing complaints that the sinner and the backslider have against our modern churches, that when they go to church no one seems to care, no one shakes hands with them, no one seems glad to see them.

A seventeen-year-old boy in Waxahachie, Texas, told Mrs. Rice that no one had ever in his life talked to him about being a Christian. His mother and father were church members, he had often attended Sunday school and church and revivals, and yet no one had ever urged him to trust in Christ and be saved. Surely it must have been that no one cared very much.

Several years ago I lived in Ft. Worth on Seminary Hill, and made that my headquarters as an evangelist. In the Southwestern Baptist Theological Seminary located there, I had taken my training. Mrs. Rice and I often attended the Seminary Hill Baptist Church (now the Gambrell Street Baptist Church). Mrs. Rice attended a class for women taught by Mrs. Scarborough, a fine teacher, whose illustrious husband had been president of the Seminary for many years. He was a great soul winner, an earnest man of God, and his wife a blessed, good Christian. In the class was an unsaved woman. My wife became concerned about her and said to me one day, "Will you go with me to see this lost woman and try to win her?" I agreed to go, but with a great deal of anxiety. The lost woman lived among preachers. Her next-door neighbor on one side was a preacher, I think; on the other side lived a Christian educational worker. Three or four doors away lived the president of the Seminary. I lived not far away, and so did many other preachers. This unsaved woman had been at-

24

tending the services. I felt that surely she must be gospel-hardened. It seemed to me likely that she had been approached many, many times about her soul in that warm evangelistic atmosphere. With some dread we prepared to go visit her and try to win her to Christ. My wife engaged a woman to stay with the children a whole afternoon, and after prayer we went to call on the unsaved woman, prepared for a long and hard battle to win her to Christ.

She met us at the door with a friendly smile. She seemed pleased that we had come to see her. We are so often cowards when we come to speak about Christ, and that afternoon I looked about me to find some point of contact that I might come gradually to the question of salvation. On the table I saw a nice new Bible, and I commented upon it. She said, "Yes, my mother gave me that last Christmas." Then I said, "I understand you are not a Christian. Wouldn't it be wonderful if you were a Christian, so that you and your husband could read the Word of God together every night?" Her face was very grave as she answered, "We are not Christians, but we do read the Bible every night. Every night since last Christmas we have read a chapter in this new Bible."

I was somewhat taken back and nonplused, so I started over again, and said, "But if you were a Christian, when you read this Bible you and your husband could get down together and pray, and ask God to bless you and lead you right and keep you safe through the night. Wouldn't it be fine to be a Christian and have family prayer?"

Her lips trembled. Tears came into her eyes as she said, "I'm not a Christian, but we do pray. Every night my husband and I read a chapter in this Bible, and then get down on our knees and pray."

I hardly knew what to say. Here was a woman whom I had supposed was gospel-hardened. I supposed that many, many times she had turned down the Saviour. Living in the midst of Christians and special workers, I thought that surely she must have been urged many times to trust in Christ. But instead of being hardened, she and her husband were daily reading the Bible and praying. And even then she was in tears! So I left off all devices and plainly asked the question, "Then why is it that you have turned down Jesus? Why is it you are not a Christian?" Breaking out into sobbing she said, "I *want* to be a Christian, but I don't know how!"

My heart was stirred. To my shame I found that right here, a few blocks away from me, was a woman who daily read the Bible and prayed and tried to find God. Around her were preachers and their wives and others dedicated to lifetime Christian work as gospel singers, Christian education workers and missionaries. All of us were occupied with our own business and never took time to tell this lost woman how to be saved.

I took up that new Bible and said, "Well, God bless you; you are going to find out how to be saved." I turned to the third chapter of John and read the wonderful story about how one must be born again, how God loves sinners, and how those who believe in Christ have everlasting life and shall never perish. In five minutes she was a happy, rejoicing Christian.

This incident has come back to my mind many and many a time to remind me of this question, "Do you really care about sinners?" We are so professional, so formal, that we let people all around us go to Hell because we do not really care. If we had a broken heart over sinners as the dear Saviour had, if we went forth weeping to find those who need the Saviour, we would feel responsible to find out those who were lost. Many are hardhearted and indifferent. Many do not want to discuss their sad, lost condition, and Jesus Christ, the remedy. But if we go with tears and hearts full of tender love for sinners for whom Jesus died, we will find those who can be saved and who ought to be saved.

How shameful it will be for many Christians, when they hear the plaintive cry of lost sinners at the judgment of God, as they say: "No man cared for my soul"! (Ps. 142:4). I know that all who reject Christ are wicked sinners and without excuse. Men ought to seek the Saviour and find Him, for He is not far from every penitent heart. But I know also that any Christian who does not love and seek sinners is without excuse. He is untrue to His Saviour, ungrateful for his own salvation, and disobedient to the Great Commission that God has given him. May God give us tender, broken hearts and weeping eyes, as we go out to win souls.

26

Nothing in this world will take the place of tears. Tears touch the heart of God. He said to Hezekiah, "I have heard thy prayer, I have seen thy tears: behold, I will add unto thy days fifteen years" (Isa. 38:5). If tears touch the heart of God, we may be sure that they somehow make a way into the hardest human hearts. Nothing proves a soul winner's sincerity like his broken heart, his tearful concern. I well know that there is a difference in my preaching when God gives me a heavenly compassion for sinners, until I cannot keep back the tears; until I yearn over sinners in the tenderest, brokenhearted anxiety. "He that goeth forth and weepeth," the Scripture says, is the man who will come back rejoicing with his sheaves. The broken heart is indispensable for the soul winner. And if you do not have a broken, tender heart, a concern for sinners, and tears over their lost condition, then I suggest that you wait before God, until the Holy Spirit gives you this Christlike concern, this shepherd heart to seek the lost ones. Wait before the Lord, until He gives you tears out of His boundless, world-embracing, brokenhearted love for sinners! Then go forth with tears.

The Word of God in Soul Winning

The soul winner must go forth not only weeping, but "bearing precious seed." The Saviour in the parable of the sower tells us, "The seed is the word of God" (Luke 8:11). This is the precious seed that the soul winner must carry, if he would come back with sheaves.

How important it is that we take the good seed, the only seed that has the divine power to spring up in the human heart with the fruit of salvation! The would-be soul winner must know ahead of time that he cannot win souls by human wisdom, human influence, personal magnetism, or tact. He goes not to reform men, but to save them. A reformation might take place without a supernatural, divine act in the heart. Men have been known to leave off drinking, cursing, or even a career of crime, under the moral influence of some strong character or some great life. But I must remind you now that that is not salvation. Unless there is a supernatural change of heart, a regeneration, a new birth, the sinner is still a lost sinner, a rejecter of Christ, a rebel against God,

27

justly condemned and Hell-bound. Admit it now, dear soul winner, you must have heavenly help in this business of saving sinners. "For the weapons of our warfare are not carnal, but mighty through God to the pulling down of strong holds" (II Cor. 10:4). You must take supernatural weapons for this warfare, supernatural seed for this sowing. You must take the living, supernatural Word of God. "For the word of God is quick, and powerful, and sharper than any twoedged sword, piercing even to the dividing asunder of soul and spirit, and of the joints and marrow, and is a discerner of the thoughts and intents of the heart" (Heb. 4:12). Remember the word of God to Jeremiah, "Is not my word like as a fire? saith the LORD; and like a hammer that breaketh the rock in pieces?" (Jer. 23:29).

Depend upon the Word of God to bring conviction. You cannot out-talk a sinner. Do not depend upon long, drawn-out arguments. Place your dependence upon the sharp Word of God. This is holy seed and within every verse there is the germ of eternal life. The soul winner must have confidence in the living Word of God. It is inspired of God. It is eternally correct. The Word of God reveals every sinner's condition. It shows the love of God. Its promises are so faithful that faith comes by hearing the Word of God. If you go forth weeping, sowing this seed, you may expect a blessed harvest.

The soul winner ought to learn by memory many, many Scriptures. He should saturate himself in the message of the Word of God. He should speak in terms of the Word. He should surrender himself to the Holy Spirit who is the author of the Word. When the Spirit wields the Sword of the Spirit, then a mighty work is done.

Often, some wife has said, "O Brother Rice, I hope you can say something that will touch my husband's heart." Let us not think that illustrations, logic, songs or poems will win souls. These are useful and blessed of God only as they carry the *Word*, and as they shed light and understanding upon the Word of God. Blessed is the soul winner who quotes a Scripture, or better yet, who points out a suitable Scripture to a sinner and has him read it. There are Scriptures to fit every case, and the well-prepared, Spirit-led soul winner will use the Word of God with mighty effect.

28

Once in our home a group agreed to pray while a young woman went to see a girl friend to win her to Christ. We prayed until we were assured that God had heard, and then I went to find the young women—the soul winner and the sinner. When I found them, the lost girl stood in a kitchen door looking at John 5:24 in a Testament held open before her face by the Christian young woman.

As it dawned upon her that by simply receiving Christ she could have everlasting life and never lose it, the dear girl said, "Oh, I never knew that was in the Bible; I did not know it was as easy as that!" Tearfully, she trusted the Saviour and all of us rejoiced together. The Word of God did the work. Dear soul winner, as you go and weep over sinners, take with you the precious Word of God. It is the seed, the power of God unto salvation to every one who believes.

The Certainty of Results

The Scripture says, "He that goeth forth and weepeth, bearing precious seed, shall *doubtless* come again with rejoicing, bringing his sheaves with him." There is a certainty about results when we go in God's way. God's plans are infallible. Anybody in the world can be a soul winner, if be is willing to go in the way God has laid out here in His Word. The word *"doubtless"* here means without any doubt in the world.

I know that you will not win every sinner you approach. You may have to plead with ten sinners to win one, or with a hundred to win ten, or with a thousand to win a hundred. When the sower of whom Jesus spoke went forth to sow, some seed fell by the wayside and was carried away by the birds without sprouting. I know that many sinners will never listen seriously to the gospel. Satan takes the seed out of the heart before it has time to take root. Other seed fell among stones. Some hearts are too hard, it seems, for the Word of God to take any permanent root. In other sad cases where people receive the Word it is so choked by the cares of this world and the deceitfulness of riches that it brings no fruit to perfection. We need not expect that every sinner to whom we talk will be saved. But, thank God, some seed will fall in good soil and bring forth fruit, some thirty, some sixty and some an hundredfold.

29

Did you ever "drop corn" on the farm? If so, you planted two, three, or four grains of corn in each hill. Only one good stalk of corn is desired in a hill, but a crow may get one seed and a cutworm another, and some seed will not sprout. So to insure a good stand, one must use more seed than he expects to come to full fruitage. The cotton planter plants cotton seed thickly in a row, and when it comes up it is thinned out to a proper stand. Not every seed comes to mature fruitage, but the one who uses plenty of good seed makes a crop.

The soul winner should know ahead of time that he will have disappointments. We will never win all the lost to Christ. "Wide is the gate, and broad is the way, that leadeth to destruction, and many there be which go in thereat" (Matt. 7:13). More people will be lost than will be saved. We will never get the world converted. But the soul winner who goes forth weeping, bearing precious seed, will snatch some brands from the burning. He will come back with his sheaves.

If you go out to seek lost people, you will find some are not at home, others will not listen. A thousand hindrances will prevent the consummation of your purpose. But where one family has moved, you will find another with lost members. Where one will not hear, you will find somebody else eager for the message. You may have to turn from the rich to the poor, from the merry to the sad, before you find a willing audience for your message. You may have to turn from your own loved ones and your unsaved family to find a stranger. If those about you will not hear you, you may have to go to those in the hospitals and jails. But you may be sure that "he that goeth forth and weepeth, bearing precious seed," shall certainly come back with souls. It will take going, it will take a broken heart, and it will take the life-giving Word of God, but this combination never fails.

Going forth with weeping, sowing for the Master,
Though the loss sustained our spirit often grieves;
When our weeping's over, He will bid us welcome,
We shall come rejoicing, bringing in the sheaves.

The Soul-Winner's Joy

When one goes forth and weeps, and bears precious seed and comes back with sheaves, then how fitting that divine

30

inspiration should say, he shall "doubtless come again with *rejoicing*, bringing his sheaves with him."

There is no joy like the soul-winner's joy. The shepherd who comes home with the one lost sheep, "calleth together his friends and neighbours, saying unto them, Rejoice with me; for I have found my sheep which was lost." The woman who loses a piece of silver and finds it, "calleth her friends and her neighbours together, saying, Rejoice with me; for I have found the piece which I had lost." And when the prodigal son comes back to the father, they kill the fatted calf and the happy home is marked by a feasting and rejoicing over the boy which "was dead, and is alive again; he was lost, and is found."

So we are told that "likewise joy shall be in heaven over one sinner that repenteth, more than over ninety and nine just persons, which need no repentance"; and again, "Likewise, I say unto you, there is joy in the presence of the angels of God over one sinner that repenteth." It is only fitting that they that sow in tears should reap in joy, and so when we share the compassionate heart of the Saviour, God allows us to share, too, the joy which is in the presence of the angels. It was the soul-winner's joy that Jesus had in mind when He was willing to die for sinners. He "for the joy that was set before him endured the cross, despising the shame" (Heb. 12:2). He had in mind the joy of reaping.

In the marvelous fifty-third chapter of Isaiah, where we are told that Jesus would bear our iniquities and that with His stripes we should be healed, because He would pour out His soul unto death, we are told, too, that "He shall see of the travail of his soul, and shall be satisfied." Therefore, the Lord Jesus will come rejoicing, bringing in the sheaves, and all that have had a part in the sowing and a share in His weeping will rejoice with Him, "when the saints go marching in." When 'many shall come from the east and west, and shall sit down with Abraham, and Isaac, and Jacob, in the kingdom of heaven,' what a time of rejoicing that will be for all who sowed the precious seed and watered it with tears!

Others have the fame and plaudits of this world. Let Congress make the laws, and a New Deal President override the Constitution, and let vulgar and immoral movie stars have the limelight in the nation's press, but when the soul winner who went forth after sinners, and wept over them, and planted in their hearts the Word of God—when the soul winner comes back with the drunkard saved and made sober, or with the harlot made pure and clean, or even with a little child transformed into a child of God by being born again, the soul winner has the best of the bargain. And if we catch some gleams of joy here in the midst of our weeping, oh, what a joyful reaping when the Saviour comes and gathers up His jewels, and we see for the first time the fulness of our reaping!

The soul winner then must take the long look, and by faith look forward to the happy time when he will be paid a hundredfold for all his tears, all his sorrows, and all his self-denials.

Christian, if you are defeated, discontented, unhappy; if you have lost the joy of the Lord and you do not enjoy prayer and the Bible and Christian service as you once did, then what you need to do is to give yourself with a holy abandon to going after sinners, weeping, bearing precious seed. When you come back, as you doubtless will, the Scripture says, with sheaves, then you will come with rejoicing. Lost joy will be restored to the Christian who wins souls.

Just now the morning mail comes and with it a letter, enclosing a copy of my booklet, *What Must I Do to Be Saved?* with a decision slip signed. The man who signs his name as taking Christ as his personal Saviour says in the letter, "This pamphlet was handed to me by Mr. F. W. W——, and he insisted that I read every word, which I did." And just now I feel part of the joy I have been talking about over a sinner saved. There is no joy like coming back with sheaves.

Here is God's way of winning souls, and here are the divinely appointed results, so let us put in practice this precious verse: "He that goeth forth and weepeth, bearing precious seed, shall doubtless come again with rejoicing, bringing his sheaves with him."

SWORD of the LORD
PUBLISHERS
P. O. BOX 1099, MURFREESBORO, TN 37133

ISBN 0-87398-771-3

Printed in U.S.A.

35¹⁰

50¢/771-3